PROTOCERATOPS

by Janet Riehecky
illustrated by Diana Magnuson

THE CHILD'S WORLD

MANKATO, MN

*Grateful appreciation is expressed to
Bret S. Beall, Research Consultant,
Field Museum of Natural History, Chicago,
Illinois, who reviewed this book to
insure its accuracy.*

Library of Congress Cataloging in Publication Data

Riehecky, Janet, 1953-
    Protoceratops / by Janet Riehecky ; illustrated by Diana Magnuson.
        p. cm. — (Dinosaur books)
    Summary: Describes both known and hypothesized information about
the dinosaur Protoceratops, including its physical appearance and
lifestyle.
    ISBN 0-89565-634-5 (library binding)
    1. Protoceratops—Juvenile literature.   [1. Protoceratops.
2. Dinosaurs.]   I. Magnuson, Diana, ill.   II. Child's World (Firm)
III. Title.   IV. Series: Riehecky, Janet, 1953-   Dinosaur books.
QE862.O65R537   1990
567.9'7—dc20   90-2514
                                                                    CIP
                                                                    AC

PROTOCERATOPS

It's hard to imagine what the world was like millions of years ago when the dino-saurs lived.

Did the earth shake as dinosaurs charged across the plains?

Did the trees sway as big dinosaurs
walked past?

Would a lake overflow if a herd decided
to take a swim?

Would little dinosaurs hide until the coast was clear?

And did the insects buzz around hoping
they were too small to be noticed?

There's a lot we can only imagine about the dinosaur's world, but there is also a lot we know. Whenever scientists find dinosaur bones, teeth, footprints, or eggs, they learn something about the dinosaurs and their world.

Scientists have learned a lot about a dinosaur called Protoceratops (pro-to-SAIR-uh-tops). In the 1920's scientists found more than a hundred skeletons of this dinosaur in Mongolia. The skeletons showed what Protoceratops looked like at many different ages, from tiny babies to full-grown adults.

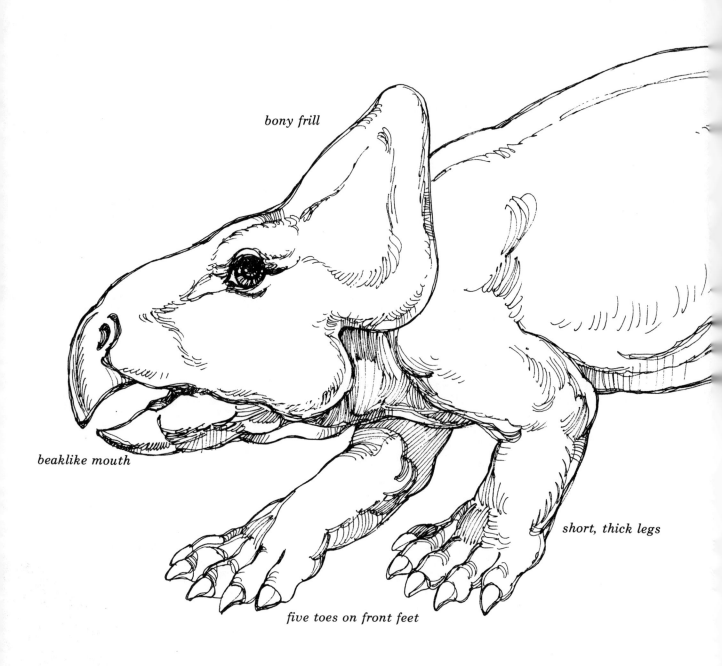

bony frill

beaklike mouth

short, thick legs

five toes on front feet

Adult Protoceratops were small for dinosaurs. They were only about two-and-a-half feet tall and six-and-a-half feet long. But they packed a lot of weight into that small body. The Protoceratops could weigh three or four hundred pounds!

short, thick tail

four toes on back feet

The adults had large, bony frills covering their heads and necks. Scientists think the frill was larger on the male than on the female. The dinosaurs' back legs were slightly longer than their front legs, and their tails were short, but strong.

The site the scientists found in Mongolia was a nesting ground. It showed that the Protoceratops laid eggs in a sandy desert area. When it was time for the female Protoceratops to lay eggs, each dinosaur

hollowed out a small nest in the sand. It laid eggs in a circle in the nest and then covered them with sand to keep them warm. The average nest had about twenty eggs in it—laid in two layers.

The Protoceratops' eggs were very small—six to eight inches long, with rough shells. The babies, which were about twelve inches long, were curled up inside. When a baby was born, it looked much like an adult, except that the frill on its head was quite tiny. But the frill—and everything else—soon grew!

The mouth of the Protoceratops had a beak and two small teeth at the front. The cheeks had many more teeth. The adult's beak and strong jaws were good for chewing tough plants, but the babies would have had a hard time chewing much of anything. Scientists think the babies stayed in their nests and that adult Protoceratops chewed up plants and fed the soft mush to the babies.

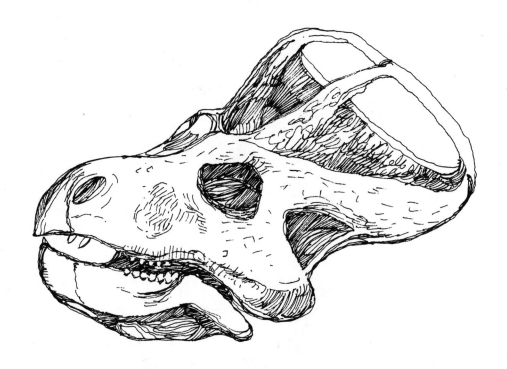

Life was dangerous for a Protoceratops even before it was born. There were many dinosaurs that loved eggs—for breakfast, lunch, or dinner!

A meat eater, such as the "egg thief" Oviraptor (O-vih-RAP-tor), might wait until a mother Protoceratops went to get some food. Then, with the coast clear, it might sneak up to the nest and dig in the sand.

When an Oviraptor found an egg, it crushed the shell with its sharp beak and

gobbled the tasty liquid inside. But sometimes it got caught during its feast. If the mother Protoceratops hadn't gone too far away, the Oviraptor would be in big trouble. Mama would charge to the rescue. The Oviraptor might have time to run away, but not always. Scientists found one Protoceratops' nest with the skeleton of an Oviraptor in it. It seems likely that the "egg thief" got caught!

Some meat eaters—bigger than Oviraptor—didn't mind meeting up with a mother Protoceratops— or even a father. To most meat eaters, an adult Protoceratops probably looked like a feast on feet. It was small, but nice and fat. Even better, it didn't have any horns or claws with which to defend itself. It couldn't even run very fast, because its legs were too short.

But it wasn't quite as easy to make a meal of a Protoceratops as it seemed. A Protoceratops wouldn't go down without a fight. And a battle between a Protoceratops and a meat eater could be very fierce indeed.

The Protoceratops could slap the meat eater with its thick, strong tail or bite it

with its sharp beak. If the meat eater bit
back anywhere on the Protoceratops'
head, it didn't hurt the Protoceratops. The
meat eater just broke its teeth on the Protoceratops' bony frill. The meat eater's
best chance was to slash at the Protoceratops' unprotected belly. But even
then it could still lose.

Scientists found skeletons embedded in rock of a Protoceratops and a meat eater called Velociraptor (veh-law-sih-RAP-tor) locked in just such a fight. The Velociraptor had grabbed the frill of the Protoceratops to hold it tight while it slashed with its claws at the Protoceratops' chin and throat. The Protoceratops was sinking its beak into the Velociraptor's stomach. Both animals seem to have died at the same time. Nobody won that fight.

At right: fossilized skeletons of Protoceratops and Velociraptor embedded in rock (copied from an actual photo)
Above: scientists' restoration of what the Protoceratops and Velociraptor looked like at the moment of their deaths.

The name Protoceratops means "first horned face." That seems a strange name for a dinosaur that didn't have any horns on its face or anywhere else. But scientists named Protoceratops "first horned face" because they think that Protoceratops was the ancestor of all the great horned

dinosaurs. Every Protoceratops had a bump on its nose, and some Protoceratops had bumps over their eyes. Scientists think that, as millions of years passed, those bumps became horns. They also think that the bony frill became larger and fancier.

The great horned dinosaurs that lived after Protoceratops were huge creatures. They had many long, dangerous horns—some even had horns on their frills!

A Protoceratops would only have come up to the knee of most of the great horned dinosaurs. And its whole body wasn't as long as the frill on some of them. But all of them could be considered the great-great-grandchildren of Protoceratops.

The Protoceratops all died long before the end of the age of dinosaurs. But their descendants, the great horned dinosaurs, were among the last dinosaurs to live on the earth.

 **Dinosaur Fun**

You can make a dino-mobile to hang in your room. You will need:

— a coat hanger
— string
— several pieces of heavy paper or thin cardboard
— crayons or markers

1. Draw the outlines of 3 to 5 of your favorite dinosaurs on the paper or cardboard. You can draw from the diagrams in the books in this series. Cut out the dinosaurs and color both sides of each with crayons or markers.
2. Punch a hole near the top middle of each dinosaur. Tie one end of a piece of string through the hole and the other to the hanger. Make each piece of string a different length so the dinosaurs will hang at different levels.